Cast Away

Caroline Pitcher
Illustrated by Peter Dennis

A & C Black · London

For Lauren

Chapter One

It was so dark out there! The sea boomed. The wind whined around the window, as if it was looking for a way in. I could hear Laura snoring on the top bunk. Yasmin grabbed my arm.

Someone's outside!

6

I had to turn that handle. The door creaked open. The corridor was pitch black, but there was a mass that seemed blacker than the rest. I could hear soft breathing.

Who's that?

Someone was whispering.

I want to talk to Laura.

8

I knew Laura would kill me if I didn't wake her, so I shook her shoulder.

Wakey! Dean is here, Dean so Mean and Lean.

She sat up at once and pushed her hair back from her bleary eyes.

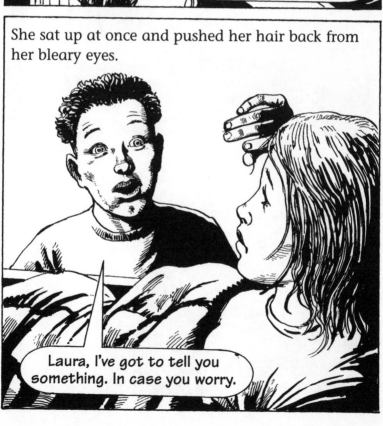

Laura, I've got to tell you something. In case you worry.

9

10

11

He blew a kiss and was gone.
Laura fell down out of her bunk and pulled at a tangle of clothes.

14

But I need a friend as well, Kate.

I looked at Yasmin, who gave me one of her 'I told you so' looks.

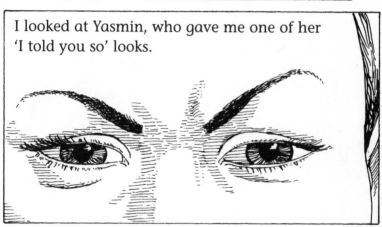

I sighed. I began to pack my shoulder bag.

All right. I'll come too.

Laura's face lit up like a Christmas tree.

Yes, that's right. All three of us went to Skull Island in the middle of the night.

Chapter Two

In the distance the sea churned and boomed.
I thought, it's like a giant washing machine. Most of
a moon hung in the sky and bathed the wet beach
with silver. Three eerie lights were bobbing and
weaving ahead of us.

Suddenly a bright circle of light shone right into
my face!

Stop it, James!

It wasn't really called Skull Island. That was James. He'd named it Skull Island that morning. Its real name was East Rock, or something. It was bleak, though – just a heap of old rocks, gleaming pale and smooth and skull-like in the moonlight. You could only go there when the tide was out.

No one spoke. I glanced back at my footprints. They shivered wetly, then vanished. They'd vanish soon anyway, when the sea came up again.

21

And the ghosts.

Just saints and hermits on these islands. No ghosts, Yasmin.

Yes ghosts, James.

Her voice was oh-so-small in that big wild space.

23

So why was there a wobble in his voice?

Chapter Three

Yasmin tucked her arm in mine. She was shivering.

> I don't like this, any of this.

> Don't fret, girl. All that has to happen now is Lean Mean Dean gets his stupid camera from the top of the rocks.
> Then we can go back and get into our nice hard bunk beds.

> But what if Miss Stephens and Mr Williams find we're missing?

Dean didn't look too keen, I must say.

27

He was smirking. Now, I must tell you something. I used to be big friends with James Jenner. Just for a little while. But he boasts. He shows off. And he always has to have the last word.

We trained the torches on the rocks as Dean began to climb. In the moonlight the rocks glistened. They must have been wet from the spray.

Not much of a mountain goat, are you, Dean?

Dean kept slipping and sliding, and stones cascaded from his feet.

Silly, *climbing* in trainers.

Yasmin says that they competed all the time when they were younger, James and Dean.
Big sigh from James. He seemed to think he was in some kind of film, a hero, with a white vest and leather wristlets with studs.

Go on then, Macho Man Jenner. You do it!

Laura gets so irritated when James puts her dear Dean down.

All right, then, I will!

He started to climb.

And then it happened. James flapped his arms, did a kind of floppy-haired dance for a second. He looked like a demented scarecrow.

Then he fell.

He took a long time to fall.
He slipped and slithered and snatched at a clump of sea-pinks but it was no good.

He couldn't stop.
Until he landed at the bottom.

In the moonlight his face looked blue. He was groaning. I crouched near, but I couldn't understand what he said.

The others just stood there as Dean made it down on his own, staring at the heap formerly known as James Jenner.

I heard myself saying this. How stupid I sounded! I was thinking, concussion, punctured lung, perforated stomach, tangled up intestines...

But I knew it wasn't all right at all...

Chapter Four

Adam always has everything, you see. Every computer game going, his own telly, pager, mobile phone. Speechlessly he handed me the phone.

The phone wouldn't work.

We did. He was groaning and writhing around now, clutching his leg.

The sea had slid secretly, swiftly round the island and over the sands. We were cut off.

Adam snatched the whistle from Yasmin and blew it as hard as he could, again and again. But the wind just picked up the sound and carried it far out to sea.

All right.
What about a flare?
A raft? A flag?
Your shirt would make a flag, Dean!

Oh yeah, Superbrain! How's about a message in a bottle? The QE2?

So have you got a better idea, Dean?

I took my shoulder bag and tucked it under James's head to make him more comfortable. He grunted. I could feel tears coming, so I turned from them all and walked away.

What a difference a few hours make...

A few hours ago we'd all been on this island, the whole class, looking at bits of rock with Miss Stephens and Mr Williams.

We'd seen puffins with clowns' noses, cormorants and terns.

We'd paddled in the rock pools like little children, finding touchy pink anemones and crabs waving a claw from inside a shell.

We'd pulled out bead-curtains of seaweed, the kind that goes pop when you squeeze the bubbles.
We'd even made a sandcastle and had such a laugh.

It seemed years ago. And now we were cast away. And no one knew.

How high does the tide come?
We'll all be drowned!

Chapter Five

I ran back to warn them.

They'd all gone! There was only James, lying on the rocks, moaning and muttering to himself.

Where are they?

James, where is everyone?

Dunno. What are you going to do? How are you going to get me back?

What do you mean, how am I going to get you back? What about your macho SAS friends?

I could hear my own voice getting squeaky with panic. He shrugged and then winced. I felt mean. After all, he was in pain.

Then I heard something odd. What was it?
Something horrible...

I remembered Limpet Stores (with the E and the T falling off). A very lame shop indeed. I remembered us buying sad shell animals and sweet pink rock. I'd love to be outside Limpet Stores now!

So one was sick, another had disappeared, the third couldn't walk. What about the other two, Dean and Laura?

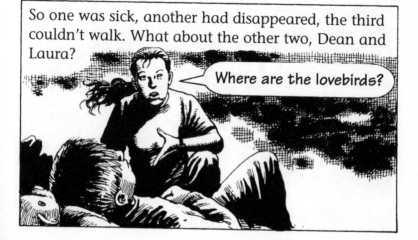

45

> Gone back.

> What do you mean, gone back?
> They can't. They –

I stared towards the distant shore of the mainland.
There were two people in the sea. Wading out,
holding hands.

They didn't hear me. As I watched, one of them suddenly vanished under the water! I tell you, Adam wasn't the only one who felt sick.

Chapter Six

So in I went. The water was so cold it stopped my breath. How could it have got so deep so quickly? And it was so strong! It swelled and shifted, it wanted to drag my legs away!

I heard my breath pounding in my ears as I struggled towards them, slow motion. Suddenly my feet left the bottom and I was adrift!

Get control, girl!

49

I swam as strongly as I could...

...and came up against Laura's terrified face.

Dean's face burst out of the water.

Dean coughed and spluttered, and I tell you, part of me wanted to laugh.

From somewhere at the back of my brain surfaced that life-saving stuff I'd learned years ago.
But we saved lives in the swimming-pool, not the North Sea.

Water surged over my face and left me with sea in my mouth and lungs.

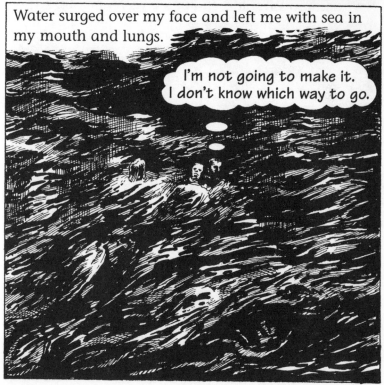

I'm not going to make it. I don't know which way to go.

Kate! This way. Kate! Keep going! It's all right!

At once I felt better. James's voice helped me to focus on where I was going.

Never did minutes last so long. Five years later the three of us collapsed on the pebbly island shore.

You – can't – swim, Dean! You put – ALL – of us in danger!

I crawled over to James and pulled at my bag. My numb fingers fumbled with the fasteners.

I've still got my disgusting packed lunch.

Now it looked delicious, that limp bread filled with oily fish paste. There were a couple of spongy brown apples, a blackened banana and some deformed chocolate biscuits. James had squashed them with his great big head. Like me, Laura and Dean were wet through and shivering.

I took an extra huge bite into a sandwich.
It was disgusting, but it was food.
Poor James watched hungrily.

Thank you for calling out to me, James.
I just followed your voice and I was safe!
I'm sorry you can't have anything to eat,
really I am.

What's happened to Adam and Yasmin?
There should be six of us, not four.

Shut up, Jenner! This is all your fault, you —

Stop it both of you. It's nobody's fault. You're wasting time! We're trapped here, the tide is still rising, and we'll all be thrown out of school for this. If we don't drown first.

57

Chapter Seven

All right, we shouldn't have moved James. But what were we supposed to do? Leave him to drown as the water level rose? He whimpered as we lifted him and my heart flipped, I didn't like to hear him in pain. It hurt me too.

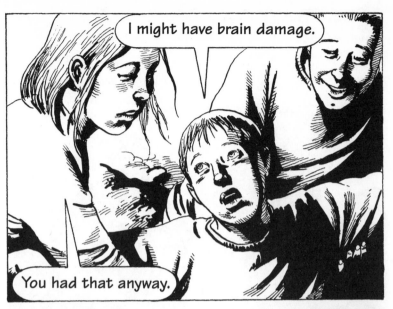

Adam appeared from round the rocks.

How should I know? Have you got any bright ideas?
Hot air balloon? I know! We can put a message in a bottle.
We haven't got a bottle.
Don't remind me how thirsty I am! Did anyone else see that lightning? That's all we need.

I hadn't heard any thunder, but then there was another flash which made us jump. I hate storms, they frighten me. As if I wasn't frightened enough already.

Does anyone know where Yasmin's got to?

The others just shrugged.

I'm going to find her, you lot stay here.

There's not much else we can do, Kate!

I was careful as I climbed. Very careful. Soon I was at the top of the rock. I didn't dare stand up. I thought of home, thought of Mum and Dad and Jonathan and Sarah, and our cat Chester, all sitting on the sofa watching Animal Hospital and eating chocolate Hobnob biscuits. I felt so alone...

And then guess what I heard? Sad sorrowful cries. Haunting, lost cries. They're seagulls I told myself.

And then I looked at the waves. My heart skipped a beat.

Ghosts!

A hand touched my shoulder.

AAAGH!

Kate! I was just coming back to find you.

I could have strangled her.

Yasmin! Where've you been?

What are they out there?

65

How could she be so calm? Hadn't she noticed the lightning? I prayed she was right. I waved the torch around and flashed it on and off and tried to remember Morse code.

And then it went out. The battery had gone.

Chapter Eight

And then I saw it. It must have been there all the time. It looked a bit like a rock, a little way off, because it was the wrong way up.

Come on, Yasmin! Help me!

Between us we turned it over. Inside lay a pair of oars! And it looked just big enough for six. Yasmin grunted as she tried to move it.

Wait, we're not strong enough. Let's get the others to help us, or we'll drop it and damage it on the rocks.

So carefully, oh so carefully, the five of us carried the boat back.

We lifted James in. He lay in the bottom.
Then we scrambled in ourselves.

> **Get off that oar, Dean.
> Sit down by Laura and stay still.**

> **Next to him, Adam.
> Kate and I will row.
> You lot would just lose it.**

And so we rowed and rowed! We were going with
the tide and the storm seemed to have died away as
soon as it started, so it wasn't too much of a struggle.

Our spirits rose as we neared the mainland.

> **Hurray! We've done it!
> We're safe at last!**

But she spoke too soon...

Now I knew why that little boat had been abandoned on the island. It had a big hole under the floor! It was filling with water and we were sinking fast.

Help! Help!

Do you know, Kate,
I think we're all going to drown.

Chapter Nine

But we didn't drown. By the time our little boat
sank to the bottom, we were in the shallows.

We lugged James back to the hostel.

We sneaked in and struggled up the stairs. We had
all agreed to hide our filthy wet clothes in our
luggage. We were going home today anyway.

Laura, Jasmin and I had just got back into our night-
clothes when we heard voices from the boys' room.

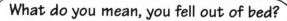

What do you mean, you fell out of bed?

I fell off the top bunk, sir. I was er – being – er –

Tarzan? An orang-utan? Stupid?

I was making a save, sir. Er – Rugby League. Yes, that's it. Dean tried to score with his sponge bag.

Mr Williams stared at them. Dean went puce in the face. We were standing behind Miss Stephens in the doorway.

Mr Williams and Miss Stephens exchanged looks.

I don't believe them, do you?

James looked at me, questions in his brown eyes, as if to say, what do you think of me?

I gave him a smile. I was so pleased he was back safely. He winked, a cheeky James wink. He must have been feeling better.

What I don't understand is all the wet on the staircase. Or the fact that Dean looks as if he's got half the beach on him. However... if a sprained ankle is the worst that's happened, I think we might turn a blind eye. Don't you think so, Eddie?

She meant Mr Williams.
Sighs of relief all round, except for one...
There's always one...

I wanted to kick him. All that terrible time, and we'd come through it, and now he had to open his great big mouth, and I almost shouted at him that we'd only gone out to Skull Island because of him. Well, all right, a lot of it was James's fault... Good job I didn't tell. That would have given the whole game away.

Never mind about that now, Dean. We'll sort out the camera business later. Good health is paramount. I'll just get my coat, then we'll drive James to Casualty. Come on, Ed – Mr Williams.

Dean's mouth hung open like a North Sea cod as Yasmin dangled the camera on its cord just out of his reach. She had the films too!

So that's what she had been doing. Everyone else had forgotten about the dare.

Yasmin smiled her sweet-as-honey smile.

That's what the lightning was! The flash from the camera. No wonder I didn't hear any thunder.

So you'd better all be nice to me because I've taken that film out. Only I know where it is!

Yasmin's face was full of mischief and delight. Their faces were puzzled. Now there were lots of gawping fish, Dean and Laura and Adam and James. Then their faces changed as they realised what she'd done. They looked furious! Can fish scowl?

You've got to laugh.

Well, James smiled, just. And I remembered what a nice smile he has.